Into Your Hands

Contemplating The Stations Of The Cross

Scott Owings

Paintings and Afterword by Dawn Whitelaw

PREFACE

Several years ago, while leading a contemplative service at the Otter Creek Church, I was approached by Dawn Whitelaw who asked me whether there was anything she could do to serve. In Dawn's quiet and humble way, she failed to mention that she was an amazingly talented and award-winning painter! In time we began to dream about a project based on the New Stations of the Cross which could be used as a guide for contemplating how to face death and life. Since their initial debut during the season of Lent, Dawn's Stations have been pondered in churches and in hospitals, with hospice patients and with teens.

As a hospice chaplain with Guardian Hospice, I've shared these Stations of the Cross with many of my patients, always amazed how the simple contemplation of hands seems to invite the dying, and the living, to more fully "let go" into the hands of God. One day, while I was showing Station One to a particular patient, he encouraged me to write some meditations and prayers to accompany Dawn's paintings. Because he was at least the third person to suggest this, I took it as a nudge from God to do just that.

Soli Deo gloria!

--Scott Owings

INTRODUCTION

In our fast-paced, high-tech world where speed and efficiency are prized commodities, noise is the norm, and suffering and death are often ignored, how does one live a happy, peaceful life?

Via Contemplatio.

Contemplation on the "Stations of the Cross" goes back to the earliest centuries of the church as "followers of the Way" wanted to retrace the steps of their Crucified Lord. In the Middle Ages—when travel to the holy city of Jerusalem became difficult—towering cathedrals were built that became sites of pilgrimage, and many walked weeks or more to come into these places that resounded with dedication, holiness, and the shared silence of the sacred path of Jesus. During this time, the Stations of the Cross became a creative, artistic tool that aided contemplation of death and life.

The Stations of the Cross are far more than an ancient relic or modern gimmick—they are a compass, a guide for the heart, and a real source for healing. The Stations offer wise counsel on how to live with dignity, grace, freedom, and a compassionate touch. They beckon to honest prayer, truthful speech, and deep listening, no matter whether one is staring death in the face or simply seeking to follow the Lord.

As you gaze upon these prints and contemplate the Spiritual Exercises, Scriptures, and Prayers, our hope is that you would be reminded of God's deep and abiding love for you, for your family friends, for your enemies, and for the whole world!

SPIRITUAL EXERCISE

Spread your fingers and hold up your palms up to your face. Gaze closely at your hands, looking at the lines and veins, along with the texture, of each hand. Take several minutes to do this, noticing also the space between your fingers.

Now, with your hands still 5-10 inches in front of your face, look beyond your hands and focus on an object 5-10 feet away. While remaining aware of your hands being close to your face, intentionally keep them in the background of your gaze.

Pause for a few moments to consider how the spiritual life is like this—that is, there is always the immediate situation and the "bigger picture."

Ask yourself, What is the biggest challenge before me right now? Honestly consider how your current health condition, an unrealized expectation, a strained relationship, or even an upcoming death can cause suffering and blind you to the bigger reality of being held in God's hands.

Take a few minutes to contemplate the "bigger picture" of your life. As best you can, try to see your immediate situation in light of the greater reality of being held by God. You might want to gaze at the picture of Jesus's hands to be reminded of his very real desire to be somewhere else—yet his trust in his Father to see him through.

STARTER PRAYER

O Lord, I feel alone and confess I can lose sight of You. I don't' wan to ignore my pain and fear while at the same time not forgetting that you are the bigger picture. Take away my fears and suffering, especially about death. Ease my doubts that no one cares or understands. With all that is within me, I desire to fix my gaze on you instead of my immediate situation. I don't want to live in denial of what I'm facing but neither do I want to be overwhelmed by my own suffering. Into your hands, O Lord, I commit my spirit. May your will be done, Amen.

MATTHEW 26:36-39

36 Then Jesus went with them to the olive grove called Gethsemane, and he said, "Sit here while I go over there to pray." 37 He took Peter and Zebedee's two sons, James and John, and he became anguished and distressed. 38 He told them, "My soul is crushed with grief to the point of death. Stay here and keep watch with me." 39 He went on a little farther and bowed with his face to the ground, praying, "My Father! If it is possible, let this cup of suffering be taken away from me. Yet I want your will to be done, not mine."

SPIRITUAL EXERCISE

Place a coin in your hands. Turn it over, smell it, feel its texture. Then take a few minutes to consider all the money that has passed through your hands over the years.

Of what are you most proud in regards to your money? What regrets do you have in terms of spending money unwisely?

Has money ever spent you?

Could it be said that money has been your god?

Now, grasp your hand tightly over the coin. How does this feel? As you continue holding the coin tightly, take a few moments to consider how you have possibly grasped too tightly onto money and/or possessions.

Finish the exercise by slowly opening your hand, quietly reflecting how you, at times, have served money more than you've served God.

STARTER PRAYER

I confess, O Lord that I have been like Judas. I have betrayed you, lusting for money, holding tightly to its seducing power. I have deceived myself thinking I could follow you and hold on tightly to money and possessions at the same time. Forgive me for betraying you, for pretending intimacy with you, all the while wanting more and more of money and the things it can buy. I desire to "let go" of my grasp on material things so that I can grasp—or rather be grasped by—you. Amen.

MATTHEW 26:47-50

47 And even as Jesus said this, Judas, one of the twelve disciples, arrived with a crowd of men armed with swords and clubs. The leading priests and elders of the people had sent them. 48 The traitor, Judas, had given them a prearranged signal: "You will know which one to arrest when I greet him with a kiss." 49 So Judas came straight to Jesus. "Greetings, Rabbi!" he exclaimed and gave him the kiss. 50 Jesus said, "My friend, go ahead and do what you have come for." Then the others grabbed Jesus and arrested him.

SPIRITUAL EXERCISE

Take your "pointer" finger and point as if you were blaming someone. To get the full effect, you might want to whisper (or shout) the words, "It's your fault."

Though this might seem like a silly exercise, consider how easy it has been to blame others for the bad fortune you have experienced. Sometimes, you may even be justified in getting angry at others, especially at institutions such as Government, Education, Schools, and Health Care for how they have not met your needs or expectations.

Next, consider how others may have blamed you for their bad fortune or unhappiness. It is hard to have someone point their finger at you, especially if it was done unfairly. As you remember people's false expectations or blame of you, take a look at the picture, remembering how Jesus was falsely accused.

Finally, consider how through the years you may have pointed the blaming finger at yourself. It is not uncommon to blame ourselves for our physical or spiritual condition, when in all likelihood we are harder on ourselves than God is.

With all this "blame game" in mind, take a few minutes to gaze at the picture once again, realizing that Jesus willingly took the blame for you. Whether your tendency has been to blame yourself or to blame others, take your "pointer finger" and lay it on your heart. Leave it there for a few minutes, aware that Jesus joyfully carried your blame and shame, and even now wants to set you free.

STARTER PRAYER

Lord, I recognize how often I have played the blame game. I have blamed others for my misfortune or failing health. I have blamed myself, at times unfairly, for the bad things that have happened in my life. On occasion, I have even pointed the finger at you, O God, accusing you falsely of not caring or being present. I place all this blame in your hands, asking for the grace to rest in you. Amen.

MARK 14:55-56

55 Inside, the leading priests and the entire high council were trying to find evidence against Jesus, so they could put him to death. But they couldn't find any. 56 Many false witnesses spoke against him, but they contradicted each other.

SPIRITUAL EXERCISE

Like Peter, all of us have blown it! Numerous have been the occasions that we have denied—by word and action—our relationship and loyalty to God. Though it can be sad and even depressing to recall our failings, to ignore or run from our mistakes can be even worse.

Take a few minutes to bow your head and place one hand on each side of your head. As best you can, get the feel of your hands. What does it feel like to embody these hands? Notice any twitching, pulsing, or sensation. Next, shift your attention to your head, noticing how it feels to have your hands placed there.

After getting a good sense of your hands and head, quietly request God to bring to your awareness some of the times you have blown it. Don't try to control your thoughts; just observe what surfaces to your consciousness.

Finally, take your hands off of your head and bring them to where you can see them with palms facing up. This simple gesture—especially when combined with using your imagination to see how Jesus has offered to receive your guilt into his hands—may bring tears, even weeping. That's okay. In fact, as with Peter, you may very well feel that these tears, along with the releasing of your denials, bring a surprising sense of healing and relief.

STARTER PRAYER

Lord Jesus Christ, Son of God, have mercy on me a sinner. I have blown it, far more than I typically care to remember. I have denied you in thought, word, and action. Forgive me for what I have done, and left undone. By your grace, turn my weeping into joy and lighten the heaviness of my head and hands, filling them once again with your loving presence, acceptance, and love. Amen.

LUKE 22:54-57

54 So they arrested him and led him to the high priest's home. And Peter followed at a distance. 55 The guards lit a fire in the middle of the courtyard and sat around it, and Peter joined them there. 56 A servant girl noticed him in the firelight and began staring at him. Finally she said, "This man was one of Jesus' followers!"

57 But Peter denied it. "Woman," he said, "I don't even know him!"

SPIRITUAL EXERCISE

We all know what it's like to have dirty hands. As a child, your hands became dirtied as you played. As an adult, you have allowed your hands to get dirty from things like soil, machines, and dishes. Dirty hands have been unavoidable and, no matter our age, we have always washed our hands to make them clean.

In the picture above, as well as in the reading, we are invited to see and remember how Pilate used his hands. Not only was Pilate responsible for binding Jesus's hands (thus taking away his freedom) he washed his own hands as a symbolic act of trying to remove his own guilt.

For this exercise, take a few minutes to consider all the occasions and ways you have sought to remove your own guilt. You may find it helpful to, like Pilate, "wash your hands" slowly and deliberately, mindful that although you can remove physical dirt from your hands, you are incapable of removing the stain of your sin.

STARTER PRAYER

Christ, my hardness of heart and fear have stained my hands. I desire to wash myself clean, realizing, however, there is nothing I can do. I also recognize that, like Pilate, I have not come to the aid of those who have been bound and falsely accused. Would you wash my hands, forgiving me and setting me free? With all that is within me, I will trust your unfailing love to make all things new! Amen.

MARK 15:4-13

4 and Pilate asked him, "Aren't you going to answer them? What about all these charges they are bringing against you?" 5 But Jesus said nothing, much to Pilate's surprise.

6 Now it was the governor's custom each year during the Passover celebration to release one prisoner—anyone the people requested. 7 One of the prisoners at that time was Barabbas, a revolutionary who had committed murder in an uprising. 8 The crowd went to Pilate and asked him to release a prisoner as usual.

9 "Would you like me to release to you this 'King of the Jews'?" Pilate asked. 10 (For he realized by now that the leading priests had arrested Jesus out of envy.) 11 But at this point the leading priests stirred up the crowd to demand the release of Barabbas instead of Jesus. 12 Pilate asked them, "Then what should I do with this man you call the king of the Jews?"

13 They shouted back, "Crucify him!"

SPIRITUAL EXERCISE

Begin this exercise by making a tight fist. Hold this grip tightly for two minutes, noticing your muscles, veins, and any sensations that occur.

After letting go, ask yourself, Have I ever used my hands to hurt another? Have I ever punched or slapped anyone? Have I ever thrown down anything with heated anger in order to make a point? Take a few minutes to gaze at one or both hands, considering how you may have used your hands to cause another pain or discomfort.

Though it may not be pleasant to recall, Jesus mentioned that the way we treat others is in essence how we treat him. Therefore, consider, once again, how you have used your hands to hurt another human being. But this time, instead of remembering a specific person that you may have hurt, consider that this was an action that hurt Jesus. That is, instead of honoring Jesus with your hands, you have, in effect, also crowned him with thorns. Allow this sober truth to sink in.

Finally, as an act of penance, tighten one of your hands into a fist again. But this time, open your fist, palm facing upward, and quietly say the Jesus Prayer: "Lord Jesus Christ, Son of God, have mercy on me, a sinner."

STARTER PRAYER

Instead of using my hands to honor and bless, I have used them with spite, even violence, to hurt others which in effect caused you pain. I am truly sorry and I humbly repent. In the days ahead, may I find a creative way to use these hands to bless those that I have harmed. Whether it be through a warm handshake, a kind hug, or a thoughtful letter or email, may I express through my hands that I want to make amends. And, if it is not possible—because of death or distance—to show my sorrow for the one(s) that I have harmed with my hands, then may I honor their memory with this prayer of my open hand.

MARK 15:16-20

16 The soldiers took Jesus into the courtyard of the governor's headquarters (called the Praetorium) and called out the entire regiment. 17 They dressed him in a purple robe, and they wove thorn branches into a crown and put it on his head. 18 Then they saluted him and taunted, "Hail! King of the Jews!" 19 And they struck him on the head with a reed stick, spit on him, and dropped to their knees in mock worship. 20 When they were finally tired of mocking him, they took off the purple robe and put his own clothes on him again. Then they led him away to be crucified.

STATION

6

JESUS CROWNED WITH THORNS

SPIRITUAL EXERCISE

Take a few moments to look at your hands and notice the possible calluses, scars, and lines. As you do so ask yourself, What is the heaviest thing I have physically carried with my hands? You might want to also consider what was involved with carrying something heavy: picking up, holding, grasping, then letting go. Quietly give thanks for what your hands have been able to lift and carry.

During Jesus' lifetime he also carried heavy things. After all, he was a carpenter, so he was certainly familiar with the weight of wood beams, even crosses. Though carrying his own cross was likely the heaviest, most excruciating thing Jesus ever did, "carrying the cross" was far more than a physical act. It was deeply symbolic, even sacramental. After all, Jesus said on more than one occasion, "If any want to become my followers, let them deny themselves and take up their cross daily, and follow me." (Luke 9:23)

The real invitation about carrying one's cross is spiritual. Therefore, take five minutes to gaze once again at your hands asking yourself, Do I really want to be a follower of Jesus? What (or whom) might I need to carry today? How can I take care of my own soul while denying myself for others?

STARTER PRAYER

O Lord, I am reminded of the words, "We are put on earth a little while to bear the beams of love." Thank you for carrying your cross, for carrying me with love and for love! This day I renew my vow to carry my cross, asking for the strength to do so with grace and love. Amen.

JOHN 19:17

17 Carrying the cross by himself, Jesus went to the place called Place of the Skull (in Hebrew, Golgotha).

STATION

JESUS CARRIES HIS CROSS

SPIRITUAL EXERCISE

With both palms facing up, bend your arms so that your left palm rests on your right forearm, and your right palm on your left forearm. Take a few deep breaths, and then consider how someone—likely your parents or a loved one—once held you as a baby in a similar position.

Spend several minutes contemplating how you were once held, cared for, and nurtured. After all you would not be here if someone did not hold you and take care of you when you were helpless.

Next, with your hands still in this cradle-like position, consider those whom you have held: children, grandchildren, family members, perhaps even pets. Be mindful that this is one of the most loving acts your hands have done—that is, holding another with care and love. Give thanks for how God has allowed you to hold, and care for, others.

Finally, end this exercise by contemplating how you, like Simon, have been given the opportunity to hold, even carry, the cross of Jesus. With open palms facing up and resting on the inside of your elbows, spend several minutes holding in prayer all those you know, love, and with whom you come into contact.

STARTER PRAYER

May all be filled with hesed (loving-kindness)

May all experience shalom (peace)

May all live in makarios (happiness)

May all enjoy libertas (freedom)

MARK 15:20-21

21 A passerby named Simon, who was from Cyrene, was coming in from the countryside just then, and the soldiers forced him to carry Jesus' cross (Simon was the father of Alexander and Rufus.)

STATION

8

JESUS HELPED BY SIMON

SPIRITUAL EXERCISE

When you face grief—whether your own or someone else's—how do you respond? Elizabeth Kubler-Ross, the well-known grief-counselor and author, claimed there are "stages of grief," beginning with shock and denial, then moving successively to anger, depression, bargaining, and finally acceptance. Although it's helpful to understand that grief is a process, this seems much too detached a perspective when one is in the midst of grief.

Closer to home, and much more comforting, is the viewpoint offered by the Psalmist, who declares to God, "You have put my tears in his bottle" (Psalm 56:8). Though this may seem strange, it was actually a cultural practice to place one's tears in a bottle. The idea seemed to be that each tear shed is precious—in fact, a gift from God.

As you ponder this Station and consider how Jesus consoled the women who grieved with their tears, remember some of the tears that you have shed. While looking at your own hands, remember that the Lord has received, and will continued to cherish, each of your tears, holding them in his hands as a gift.

STARTER PRAYER

O Sole Refuge and Sole Hope of the unhappy, to Whom we can never pray without hope of mercy, for Thy sake, and for Thy Holy Name's sake, grant me this grace, that as often as I think of Thee, speak of Thee, write of Thee, read of Thee, preach of Thee, that as often as I remember Thee, stand before Thee, offer Thee sacrifice, prayers and praise, so often may I weep, the tears welling sweetly and abundantly in Thy sight, so that tears may be my bread by day and night.
(Saint Augustine)

LUKE 23:27-32

27 A large crowd trailed behind, including many grief-stricken women. 28 But Jesus turned and said to them, "Daughters of Jerusalem, don't weep for me, but weep for yourselves and for your children. 29 For the days are coming when they will say, 'Fortunate indeed are the women who are childless, the wombs that have not borne a child and the breasts that have never nursed.' 30 People will beg the mountains, 'Fall on us,' and plead with the hills, 'Bury us.' 31 For if these things are done when the tree is green, what will happen when it is dry?"
32 Two others, both criminals, were led out to be executed with him.

SPIRITUAL EXERCISE

At the scene of the cross, people used their hands to hurt Jesus in numerous ways: offering wine mixed with myrrh, nailing him to the cross, rolling dice, placing a mocking sign above his head, wagging their fists in spiteful hatred. Take a few moments to consider how hands (yours included) have been used to cause suffering.

If that wasn't enough, keep in mind that the greatest pain for Jesus was the apparent absence of God. In other words, God appeared to be "hands off" at the cross. This pain was so great that Jesus loudly echoed the Psalmist, "My God, my God, why have you forsaken me?" While Jesus couldn't raise his fists in protest or lament, he likely would have if possible.

End this exercise by lifting your hands, perhaps even holding them as Jesus might have on the cross. Notice what it feels like to hold your hands in such a position for a few minutes. Finally, join Jesus and Psalm 22 in addressing God with the most difficult question you can muster. Remember, this is not a sign of disrespect but of great faith! After all, God can handle your lament, complaint, or blame.

STARTER PRAYER

O God, I cannot fathom the pain that Jesus felt in his hands. Like him, sometimes I wonder, Why? How long? Where are you?

I ask these questions not out of disrespect but deep trust, knowing you can and one day, will make all things clear and right.

MARK 15:22-30

22 And they brought Jesus to a place called Golgotha (which means "Place of the Skull"). 23 They offered him wine drugged with myrrh, but he refused it.

24 Then the soldiers nailed him to the cross. They divided his clothes and threw dice to decide who would get each piece. 25 It was nine o'clock in the morning when they crucified him. 26 A sign was fastened to the cross, announcing the charge against him. It read, "The King of the Jews." 27 Two revolutionaries were crucified with him, one on his right and one on his left.

29 The people passing by shouted abuse, shaking their heads in mockery. "Ha! Look at you now!" they yelled at him. "You said you were going to destroy the Temple and rebuild it in three days. 30 Well then, save yourself and come down from the cross!"

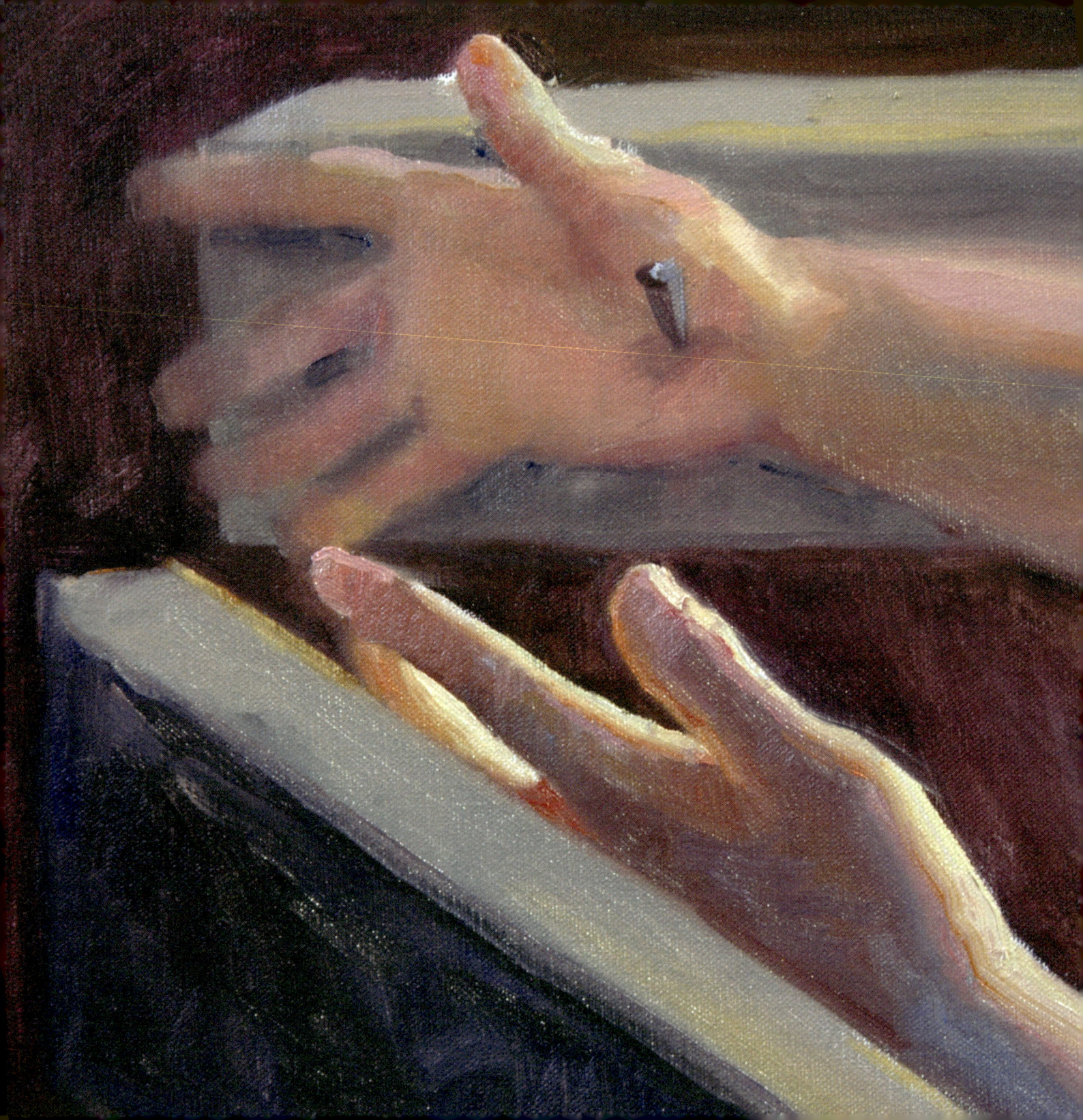

SPIRITUAL EXERCISE

It has been said that we often die as we have lived. This is certainly the case with Jesus as up to his final breath, we see and hear him blessing others.

For this exercise, place one or both hands over your heart. Take several deep breaths, noticing not only your breath but also the movement of your hands. Quietly give thanks for the gift of life.

Next, with your hands still on your heart, consider where you have been and what you have done today. Ask yourself, Have I allowed these events and people to touch my heart? If not, you might want to ask, What have I placed over my heart that would have kept me from feeling the pain, or joy, of others?

Finally, consider how Jesus, while suffering on the cross, reached out in love to the Thief on the Cross, even offering him a blessing. Although it's not always easy to speak words of blessing to others when we are feeling well, it's even more challenging when life is not treating us fairly. Despite the difficulty, and no matter how you are currently feeling, take a few moments to consider the people in your life who need a word of blessing or hope. And although you can't promise them paradise, spend a few minutes, with your hands facing outward, saying the words, "May Christ be with you."

STARTER PRAYER

Christ be with me, Christ within me, Christ beneath me, Christ behind me, Christ before me, Christ beside me, Christ to win me, Christ to comfort and restore me. Christ below me, Christ above me, Christ in quiet, Christ in danger, Christ in hearts of all that love me, Christ in mouth of friend and stranger. (Saint Patrick)

LUKE 23:39-43

39 One of the criminals hanging beside him scoffed, "So you're the Messiah, are you? Prove it by saving yourself—and us, too, while you're at it!"

40 But the other criminal protested, "Don't you fear God even when you have been sentenced to die? 41 We deserve to die for our crimes, but this man hasn't done anything wrong." 42 Then he said, "Jesus, remember me when you come into your Kingdom." 43 And Jesus replied, "I assure you, today you will be with me in paradise."

SPIRITUAL EXERCISE

Begin this exercise by placing your palms together, thumbs facing your chest and fingers pointing upward. Apply some pressure so that there is little to no space between your fingers. After a few moments, you should begin to feel the pulse in your fingers.

As you look at your fingers and feel the pulse of your middle fingers, bear in mind that you and your mother were also at one time very connected. Though two beings, you were like one. And while your mother may no longer be living, or while you may have been disconnected for a long time, spend a few moments thanking God for your mother. After all, if it wasn't for your mother, you would not be here!

Next, release your fingers and spend a few moments looking closely at both sides of your hands. Ask yourself, How have I blessed (and/or hurt) my mother with my hands, words, and actions? If she is still living, you could write her a note of thanks, give her a hug, or do some other act of kindness with your hands. If she has passed on, you can still find a way to bless her memory and influence on your life. Even if your relationship was not ideal, you can still hold up your hands and say something like, "I'm thankful you brought me into the world, and into the Lord's hands I release you."

STARTER PRAYER

Thank you Jesus for showing me how important it is to love my mother. If I can take care of my mother in some tangible way, help me to do so. If she is gone, then would you take care of her, comforting her as she once comforted me.

JOHN 19:25-27

25 Standing near the cross were Jesus' mother, and his mother's sister, Mary (the wife of Clopas), and Mary Magdalene. 26 When Jesus saw his mother standing there beside the disciple he loved, he said to her, "Dear woman, here is your son." 27 And he said to this disciple, "Here is your mother." And from then on this disciple took her into his home.

SPIRITUAL EXERCISE

Begin with your palms facing down. Slowly, begin to make a fist with each hand. Tighten your thumbs, followed by tightening each of your fingers into clinched fists. As best you can, tighten your fists as much as possible and hold the grip as long as possible.

When you can hold on no longer, slowly begin to unclasp each finger and thumb. Don't rush; rather, notice the sensation of letting go.

Life is often like this. We tend to grasp and cling and hold on to ideas, to people, and even to life. On the cross—as well as during his life—Jesus teaches another way. It is the way of "letting go." Paradoxically, this letting go, or dying, is the way to life!

Finish this exercise by contemplating, To what do I hold too tightly? Am I grasping something, or someone, to such an extent that it is causing me or others to suffer? And most important, what would happen if I "let go?"

STARTER PRAYER

Nothing in my hands I bring,

Simply to Thy Cross I cling.

(Augustus Toplady)

MATTHEW 27:45-54

45 At noon, darkness fell across the whole land until three o'clock. 46 At about three o'clock, Jesus called out with a loud voice, "Eli, Eli, lema sabachthani?" which means "My God, my God, why have you abandoned me?"

47 Some of the bystanders misunderstood and thought he was calling for the prophet Elijah. 48 One of them ran and filled a sponge with sour wine, holding it up to him on a reed stick so he could drink. 49 But the rest said, "Wait! Let's see whether Elijah comes to save him."

50 Then Jesus shouted out again, and he released his spirit. 51 At that moment the curtain in the sanctuary of the Temple was torn in two, from top to bottom. The earth shook, rocks split apart, 52 and tombs opened. The bodies of many godly men and women who had died were raised from the dead. 53 They left the cemetery after Jesus' resurrection, went into the holy city of Jerusalem, and appeared to many people.

54 The Roman officer and the other soldiers at the crucifixion were terrified by the earthquake and all that had happened. They said, "This man truly was the Son of God!"

SPIRITUAL EXERCISE

Contemplating your own death may likely be one of the most difficult but important things you can do. Even if we are advanced in years or facing a severe illness, everything in our culture discourages us from facing our own mortality. This is a shame.

For this exercise, begin by imagining that you have just a few hours to live. Whom would you call? What would you tell them?

Maybe there's a final last word, even a letter, that you could write, or dictate, to someone whom you have secretly admired. Whom would that be?

Someone will likely have the privilege of saying a few words at your graveside or memorial service. Who would you like for it to be? What would you like them to say?

End this exercise by taking several deeper than normal breaths. As you do so, quietly give thanks for the gift of breath, for the gift of life. As someone has said, you are not living on the way to dying; you are dying on the way to living.

STARTER PRAYER

In your hands, O Lord,

I commit my spirit.

MATTHEW 27:57-61

57 As evening approached, Joseph, a rich man from Arimathea who had become a follower of Jesus, 58 went to Pilate and asked for Jesus ' body. And Pilate issued an order to release it to him. 59 Joseph took the body and wrapped it in a long sheet of clean linen cloth. 60 He placed it in his own new tomb, which had been carved out of the rock. Then he rolled a great stone across the entrance and left. 61 Both Mary Magdalene and the other Mary were sitting across from the tomb and watching.

AFTERWORD

When Scott first approached me to paint the Stations of the Cross for use in a contemplative Vespers service, I was not familiar with the concept. After some research and discussion with him, I became intrigued with the idea of trying to illustrate Christ's journey to the Cross.

Traditionally the 14 Stations have been depicted as full-length figures in period costume. There are many beautiful examples of the Stations, presented in both narrative paintings and sculptures. I opted to tell the story of the events that lead up to Christ's Crucifixion from an intimate, personal view by using the images of hands. The paintings were designed to be seen close up, in low light. From a technical standpoint, the original paintings were 12" x 12", oil on canvas, with the canvas stretched over a box.

My hope has always been that someone could use these images as a vehicle for deeper prayer and contemplation. If the images provide a link to God's love and to a realization of God's gift to all of us in the death of his Son, I will be most humbled and gratified.

--Dawn Whitelaw

ACKNOWLEDGEMENTS

Lisa, for acceptance, forgiveness, and love

Alex, Eric & Joy, for being tangible reminders of grace

Randy, for kind encouragement to write

Becca & Lissa, for inspiring preaching and love-full leadership

Sister Kathleen, Ben & Gordon, for Jedi guidance into silence and meditation

Preston & Jeff, for constant prayer

Sean, for generous skill in the lay-out of this book

Christina, for clear-eyed perception

David, Greg, & Joel, for good-humored accountability

Lee & Matt, for wisdom and wit

Matt P, Andrew & Lindsey, for being artful subjects on canvas and in life

Erin, cheerleader and muse

Guardian Hospice, for making work a joy

Holy Cross Hospice in Botswana, for providing the motivation to finish this book

CPSIA information can be obtained
at www.ICGtesting.com
Printed in the USA
LVIC040506250313
325720LV00001B

* 9 7 8 0 9 8 2 4 6 2 7 6 8 *